Fascinating INSECTS

Cockroaches

Aaron Carr

www.av2books.com

LET'S READ
AV²
BY WEIGL™
ADDED VALUE • AUDIO VISUAL

Go to **www.av2books.com**, and enter this book's unique code.

BOOK CODE

N327023

AV² by Weigl brings you media enhanced books that support active learning.

AV² provides enriched content that supplements and complements this book. Weigl's AV² books strive to create inspired learning and engage young minds in a total learning experience.

Your AV² Media Enhanced books come alive with...

Audio
Listen to sections of the book read aloud.

Video
Watch informative video clips.

Embedded Weblinks
Gain additional information for research.

Try This!
Complete activities and hands-on experiments.

Key Words
Study vocabulary, and complete a matching word activity.

Quizzes
Test your knowledge.

Slide Show
View images and captions, and prepare a presentation.

... and much, much more!

Published by AV² by Weigl
350 5th Avenue, 59th Floor New York, NY 10118
Websites: www.av2books.com   www.weigl.com

Library of Congress Cataloging-in-Publication Data
Carr, Aaron.
Cockroaches / Aaron Carr.
     pages cm -- (Fascinating insects)
ISBN 978-1-4896-1038-6 (hardcover : alk. paper) -- ISBN 978-1-4896-1039-3 (softcover : alk. paper) --
ISBN 978-1-4896-1040-9 (single-user ebook) -- ISBN 978-1-4896-1041-6 (multi-user ebook)
1. Cockroaches--Juvenile literature. I. Title.
 QL505.5.C37 2014
 595.7'28--dc23
                         2014002368

Printed in the United States of America in North Mankato, Minnesota
1 2 3 4 5 6 7 8 9 0 18 17 16 15 14

032014
WEP150314

Project Coordinator: Aaron Carr   Art Director: Terry Paulhus

Weigl acknowledges Getty Images as the primary image supplier for this title.

Cockroaches

CONTENTS

Meet the cockroach.

Cockroaches are small insects. They have long flat bodies.

Cockroaches can be found all around the world.

All around the world, cockroaches live in dark, warm places.

Cockroaches are born when they hatch from eggs.

When they hatch from eggs, young cockroaches are called nymphs.

Cockroach nymphs grow very fast.

As they grow very fast, cockroach nymphs shed their skin many times.

Cockroaches have wings when they are fully-grown.

When they are fully-grown, cockroaches can fly short distances.

Cockroaches can run 5 feet in one second.

Running 5 feet in one second makes cockroaches the fastest insects in the world.

Cockroaches have different ways to talk to each other.

To talk to each other, cockroaches use touch, taste, smell, and sound.

Cockroaches eat
almost any food they can find.

Eating almost any food they can find helps cockroaches live in many places.

Cockroaches are important in nature.

In nature, cockroaches eat dead plants and animals. This helps plants grow.

COCKROACH FACTS

These pages provide more detail about the interesting facts found in the book. They are intended to be used by adults as a learning support to help young readers round out their knowledge of each insect or arachnid featured in the *Fascinating Insects* series.

Pages 4–5

Cockroaches are small insects. Insects are small animals with six jointed legs and segmented bodies with hard outer shells, called exoskeletons. Their bodies have three parts: the head, thorax, and abdomen. There are more than 4,000 species of cockroaches. The American cockroach is about 2 inches (5 centimeters) long and reddish brown. The largest cockroach is 6 inches (15 cm) long and has a 1 foot (30 cm) wingspan. Cockroaches have lived on Earth for more than 320 million years.

Pages 6–7

Cockroaches can be found all around the world. The only places cockroaches do not live are polar regions and places with an elevation higher than 6,500 feet (2,000 meters) above sea level. Most cockroach species live in environments that are warm, damp, and dark. This includes forests, caves, and brush. Some cockroaches can even live in dry places, such as deserts. Only about 30 species of cockroaches will live inside houses or other buildings.

Pages 8–9

Cockroaches are born when they hatch from eggs. They develop through three stages: egg, nymph, and adult. Most species lay eggs in a sac called an ootheca. The ootheca is outside of the mother's body in some species and inside the body in others. Some species keep the eggs inside the body without an ootheca. One species gives birth to live young, similar to mammalian reproduction. After the eggs hatch, the young cockroaches, or nymphs, look like small cockroaches with no wings.

Pages 10–11

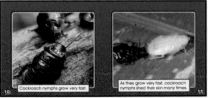

Cockroach nymphs grow very fast. When nymphs first hatch, they are white and soft. Their bodies quickly turn brown and harden. As the nymphs grow, they shed their skin several times. This is called molting. Some species develop into adults in just a few weeks, while others take more time to develop. The oriental cockroach may take more than a year to mature.

Pages 12–13

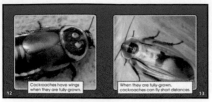

Cockroaches have wings when they are fully-grown. For most types of cockroaches, adult males have two pairs of wings and adult females either have small wings or no wings at all. However, cockroaches are not strong fliers. Male American cockroaches can only fly short distances, though they can glide farther if they start from a high place. Most of the time, cockroaches prefer to run.

Pages 14–15

Cockroaches can run 5 feet in a second. This speed earned the cockroach a spot in the Guinness Book of World Records as the fastest insect in the world. Adjusting for size differences, a cockroach running at 5 feet (1.5 m) per second is the same as a human running 200 miles (320 kilometers) per hour. At top speed, cockroaches run on their hind legs. When running at lower speeds, they use their two long antennae to feel the ground in front of them to make sure they do not run into anything.

Pages 16–17

Cockroaches have different ways to talk to each other. Most cockroaches rely on touch, taste, and smell to communicate with each other. They use their antennae to both feel for objects or other cockroaches around them and to pick up odors from the air. A cockroach can identify its family and friends by smelling them. Some types of cockroaches communicate through sound. They either hiss or rub their wings together to make noise.

Pages 18–19

Cockroaches eat almost any food they can find. They are omnivores, which means they eat both plant and animal matter. However, cockroaches have also been known to eat things such as paper and clothing. The cockroach's adaptable diet has helped it to become one of the best survivors of all animals. Cockroaches can live up to a month without eating at all, and they can survive up to a week without water.

Pages 20–21

Cockroaches are important in nature. They are decomposers. This means that they search for dead and decaying plants and animals to eat. By eating dead organic matter, cockroaches play a key role in their ecosystems. As decomposers, they help break down the dead materials and release nutrients back into the ground. This in turn helps keep soil healthy so plants can grow.

KEY WORDS

Research has shown that as much as 65 percent of all written material published in English is made up of 300 words. These 300 words cannot be taught using pictures or learned by sounding them out. They must be recognized by sight. This book contains 48 common sight words to help young readers improve their reading fluency and comprehension. This book also teaches young readers several important content words. These words are paired with pictures to aid in learning and improve understanding.

Page	Sight Words First Appearance
4	the
5	are, have, long, small, they
6	all, around, be, can, found, in, live, places, world
8	from, when
9	young
10	grow, very
11	as, many, their, times
14	feet, one, run, second
15	makes
16	and, different, each, other, sound, talk, to, use, ways
18	almost, any, eat, find, food
19	helps
20	animals, important, plants, this

Page	Content Words First Appearance
4	cockroach
5	bodies, insects
8	eggs
9	nymphs
11	skin
12	wings
13	distances
16	smell, taste, touch
20	nature

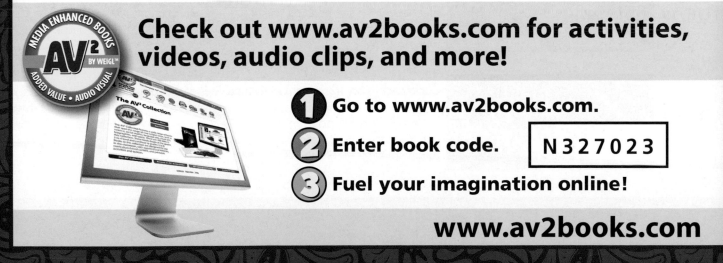